IT Governance

A Pocket Guide

IT Governance

A Pocket Guide

ALAN CALDER

IT Governance Publishing

Every possible effort has been made to ensure that the information contained in this book is accurate at the time of going to press, and the publishers and the author cannot accept responsibility for any errors or omissions, however caused. No responsibility for loss or damage occasioned to any person acting, or refraining from action, as a result of the material in this publication can be accepted by the publisher or the author.

IT Governance Publishing
IT Governance Limited
Unit 3, Clive Court
Bartholomew's Walk
Cambridgeshire Business Park
Ely
Cambridgeshire
CB7 4EH
United Kingdom

www.itgovernance.co.uk

First published in the United Kingdom in 2007 by
IT Governance Publishing.

ISBN 978-1-905356-25-6

CONTENTS

CHAPTER 1: WHY IT GOVERNANCE MATTERS

In the twenty-first century, IT governance is, within the broader corporate governance context, critical for all organizations. Those without an IT governance strategy face significant risks; those with one perform measurably better.

Governance background

The 'greed is good' business philosophy of the 1980s and 1990s seemed to give way, at the end of the twentieth century, to a 'looting is good' approach. While catastrophic financial failure is a frequent characteristic of the business cycle, widespread looting of public companies by their senior executives had become more common: BICC, Maxwell Communications, Enron and WorldCom are all good examples. The spate of collapses and financial failures at the end of the Internet bubble, though, suggested a systemic weakness whose worldwide implications included a negative knock-on effect on already problematic pension funds and pensioner assets. Shareholders are no longer enthusiastic about losses on this scale.

Governments, already grappling with the challenge of funding the pensions of an inexorably greying population bulge, started applying themselves to rooting out corporate misbehaviour. They are doing this through a combination of overt regulatory action and slightly more covert pressure on institutional investors to stand up for their rights as shareholders and more determinedly exercise their de facto responsibility to insist on proper governance from those organizations in which they have invested.

The concept of governance is a simple one: 'corporate governance is the system by which business corporations are directed and controlled'.[1] The 'holy trinity' of good corporate governance has long been seen as:

- shareholder rights,
- transparency, and
- board accountability.

While corporate governance is overtly concerned with board structure, executive compensation and shareholder reporting, the underlying assumption is that the board is responsible for directing the business and for identifying and mitigating the risks to its assets and trading future.

In today's corporate governance environment, where the value and importance of intellectual assets are significant, boards must be seen to extend the core governance principles – setting strategic aims, providing strategic leadership, overseeing and monitoring the performance of executive management and reporting to shareholders on their stewardship of the organization – to the organization's intellectual capital, information and IT.

A culture of opaqueness is out of line with today's expectation of pro-activity and governance transparency. IT is no longer merely a functional or operational issue. Directors need to be pro-active in understanding the strategic importance of, and operational risks in, intellectual capital, information and communications technology.

As younger companies, controlled and managed by people who have grown up with IT and its possibilities, transform the business landscape, so those boards that fail to respond can expect their businesses to be destroyed – and whether the destruction is piece by piece or wholesale is, in the long run, irrelevant.

---

1 OECD, *Principles of Corporate Governance*, 2004
 (*www.oecd.org/dataoecd/32/18/31557724.pdf*).

IT governance defined

IT governance is a 'framework for the leadership, organizational structures and business processes, standards and compliance to these standards, which ensure that the organization's IT supports and enables the achievement of its strategies and objectives'.[2]

In the future, IT governance will be even more important than corporate governance is today: information and IT are absolutely fundamental to business survival, and organizations that fail to 'direct and control' their IT to best competitive advantage will be left as roadkill on the information superhighway.

---

2 *IT Governance: Guidelines for Directors* (Alan Calder, ITGP, 2005, *www.itgovernance.co.uk/products/19*).

CHAPTER 2: DRIVERS FOR IT GOVERNANCE

The five major drivers of IT governance are:

1. The search for competitive advantage – in the dynamically changing information economy – through intellectual assets, information and IT.

2. Rapidly evolving governance requirements across the OECD, underpinned by capital market and regulatory convergence.

3. Increasing information- and privacy-related legislation (compliance).

4. The proliferation of threats to intellectual assets, information and IT.

5. The need to align technology projects with strategic organizational goals, ensuring that they deliver planned value ('project governance').

The information economy and intellectual capital

The new information, or knowledge, economy is fundamentally different from the old manufacturing one. The globalization of markets, products and resourcing has led to increasingly similar shopping streets selling increasingly similar products throughout the developed world. Over 70% of workers in developed economies are now knowledge, rather than manual, workers – including those factory and farm workers whose work depends on understanding and using information technology. Information networking and telecommunications connectivity make this 'global village' possible – but bring numerous threats and challenges at the same time.

The key characteristics of this global information economy are:

- Information and knowledge are not depleting resources to be protected; on the contrary, sharing knowledge drives innovation.

- Effects of location and time are diminished – virtual organizations now operate round the clock in virtual marketplaces, so that organizations based on east coast America can manufacture in China, handle customer support from India, and sell globally through a single website.

- Laws and taxes are difficult to apply effectively on a national basis as knowledge quickly shifts to low-tax, low-regulation environments.

- Knowledge-enhanced products command price premiums.

- Captured knowledge has a greater intrinsic value than 'knowledge on the hoof'.

In a very real sense, knowledge grows as it is shared; more knowledge leads to more innovation, which drives more competition, which in turn drives more globalization.

In the manufacturing economy, an organization's key asset was its productive capability: its machinery, logistical support and distribution equipment, and its stocks of raw materials and finished goods. In the information age, an organization's key asset is its intellectual capital: its human resources, retained knowledge, structural capital and intangible assets. Every organization with a long-term desire to survive and succeed in its chosen market has to focus on preserving, protecting, developing and applying its intellectual capital for the benefit of its shareholders.

Intellectual capital can be valued; in listed companies, for example, it is roughly equivalent to the difference between the market value of the company and its balance sheet net asset value.

Intellectual capital depends, for its productive existence, on information and communication technology: proper IT governance is, therefore, fundamental to both the proper governance and the long-term survival of any twenty-first century organization.

Competitiveness

IT is neither low-cost nor low-impact. It is investment-intensive. Innovation is common; speed of innovation and deployment can be critical in developing and maintaining competitive advantage. Organizations must respond pro-actively to change within their markets or see their competitive position eroded and ultimately destroyed. Schumpeter called the process 'Creative Destruction':

> '[the] process of Creative Destruction is the essential fact about capitalism... every business strategy acquires its true significance only against the background of that process and with the situation created by it. It must be seen in its role in the perennial gale of creative destruction; it cannot be understood irrespective of it or, in fact, on the hypothesis that there is a perennial lull...'[3]

IT on its own and of itself is not, however, necessarily a source of competitive advantage. The way it is used by an organization may be a source of competitive advantage but, in many situations, IT is already commoditized and organizations have to ensure that their systems and processes are as good as (or no worse than) those of their competitors, in order to ensure they don't fall behind in key performance areas.

---

3 *Capitalism, Socialism and Democracy*, Joseph A Schumpeter, 1975.

ICT makes revolutionary business models[4] possible and dramatically transforms the business environment. The challenge of online security only slows – but doesn't halt – the development of online banking, financial and other e-commerce applications.

The Internet enables small businesses everywhere to compete with larger ones, globally; digital communication speeds up outsourcing, customer awareness and reputation destruction. Instant messaging, VoIP (Voice over IP), spyware and sequential auto-responders are technologies as disruptive as CRM (Customer Relationship Management), HRM (Human Resource Management) and ERP (Enterprise Resource Planning) systems were in their day. Of course, the Internet doesn't replace the need for a real business strategy, or for generating a proper economic return for shareholders: it just transforms the environment within which the board has to create and execute strategy.

Governance convergence

The modern corporate governance movement arguably started with the Cadbury and Greenbury reports in the UK in the 1990s. They were merged into the Combined Code in December 1998 and, in 1999, the Turnbull Report provided directors with additional guidance on how to tackle internal control.

---

4 The term 'business model' '... seems to refer to a loose conception of how a company does business and generates revenue. Yet simply having a business model is an exceedingly low bar to set for building a company. Generating revenue is a far cry from creating economic value, and no business model can be evaluated independently of industry structure. The business model approach to management becomes an invitation for faulty thinking and self-delusion.'

Michael E Porter, 'Strategy and the Internet' Harvard Business Review, March 2001.

The OECD Principles of Corporate Governance were also published in 1999, but it wasn't until after Enron and WorldCom, and the US Sarbanes-Oxley response in 2002, that most other OECD countries made a determined effort to adopt codes of corporate governance. With the exception of the US though, individual OECD countries have all adopted corporate governance codes that work on the 'comply or explain' principle.

The Sarbanes-Oxley Act ('SOX') works on the basis of 'comply or be punished'. One of the impacts of SOX is that companies that are directly affected by it are requiring their partners and suppliers to certify conformance to SOX because that gives them greater certainty of ongoing compliance themselves.

Eliot Spitzer, the New York Attorney General, expressed a common view when he said:

> 'the honour code amongst CEOs didn't work. Board oversight didn't work. Self-regulation was a complete failure.'[5]

The most recent UK legislation (the 2006 Companies Act) and the current revision to the European Union's Eighth Company Law Directive on Statutory Audit point to greater compulsion – from governments, regulators and justice departments – in governance requirements becoming the norm across the OECD.

At the same time, convergence in accounting and auditing standards across the OECD, and particularly between the US and the EU, which contain the vast bulk of the world's capital markets, is driving institutional shareholders to a common framework of governance requirements.

---

5 Eliot Spitzer, interviewed in *Wall Street Journal*, 8 April 2005.

Internationally, banks also operate within a common governance and risk management framework defined by BIS (the Bank of International Settlements) and Basel 2.[6]

The requirement for all organizations to adopt best corporate governance practices, irrespective of their nationality or location, is growing stronger. The 'entry price' for access to western capital markets is, increasingly, acceptance of western accounting and corporate governance norms. These requirements cannot be met without an effective IT governance framework.

---

6 Basel Committee on Banking Supervision, *International Convergence of Capital Measurement and Capital Standards: a Revised Framework*, June 2004.

CHAPTER 3: STRATEGIC AND OPERATIONAL RISK MANAGEMENT

Risk management has always been a key governance issue. The board's job is strategy and, therefore, strategic risk has always been a board responsibility. The modern corporation's fundamental goal is to continuously create and add value to its business. This means that boards must find an appropriate balance between profit maximization and risk reduction.

Strategic risk can be described as the enterprise level risk of a negative impact on earnings or capital arising from an organization's future business plans and strategies, improper implementation of decisions, or lack of responsiveness to industry changes. It includes risks associated with plans for entering new businesses, expanding existing services, mergers, acquisitions and divestments, and enhancing the infrastructure.

Two key strategic risks related to information and communications technology are:

- interruptions to business processes and customer services, and

- overspending on IT, placing the company at a cost-disadvantage to its competitors.

Both these risks should be dealt with as part of the strategic risk management process.

In the last few years, the parallel importance of operational risk ('the risk of direct or indirect loss resulting from inadequate or failed internal processes, people and systems or from external events'[7]) has, driven by the Basel 2 process, been recognized.

---

7 'Operational Risk', a consultative document from the Basel Committee on Banking Supervision, published in January 2001.

Enterprise risk management

Risk assessment has, over the last few years, become a pervasive and invasive concept: a risk assessment must be structured and formal, and nowadays one is expected in almost every context – from a school outing through to a major corporate acquisition. It is certainly a cornerstone of today's corporate governance regimes. In the context of both strategic and operational risk, risk identification and assessment are the first steps that a board should take to controlling the risks facing the organization; the most important step is the development of a risk treatment plan (in which risks are accepted, controlled, eliminated or contracted out) that is appropriate in the context of the company's strategic objectives.

IT risk management

IT risk management has become a hot IT topic over the last few years. As organizations become increasingly dependent on information technology and intellectual capital assets, the key areas of IT risk are usually seen as:

- IT infrastructure and network security – arising from concerns about hackers, terrorists, cyber-criminals, insiders, outsiders, viruses, and so on;

- data integrity, confidentiality, privacy and compliance – arising from regulatory and market pressure around protecting both personal (eg, data protection legislation) and corporate data (eg, fair disclosure regulations), as well as financial and operational data (eg, Sarbanes-Oxley);

- business continuity – arising from concerns about the capability to continue in business after a natural or man-made disaster;

- IT management – arising from concerns about project failure, poor IT operational performance, inadequate IT infrastructure, etc.

These risks all affect more than just the IT organization within the enterprise; their impact is felt across the entire organization and they must therefore be managed within the enterprise risk management framework. IT governance ensures that IT is fully integrated into the organization, and enables the board to govern IT within the context of the overall business model, strategy and risk management framework.

Compliance risk

Information is increasingly subject to legislation. Customers, staff, suppliers, tribunals and law courts all expect organizations to proactively comply with it. There is international, foreign and industry-specific legislation and regulation. All OECD countries have some form of data protection and privacy legislation. National regulations often overlap, are sometimes contradictory, and almost all lack implementation guidance or adequate precision. Copyright, digital rights, computer misuse and electronic trading legislation are changing rapidly, and money laundering, proceeds of crime, human rights and freedom of information legislation all add to the confusion.

Complex organizations, with diversified or (partially) virtual business models, operating in and across a number of legal jurisdictions, have an even more complex task. While any one regulation (and its related compliance issues) might apply only to a subsidiary national entity, it is the global parent whose reputation might be damaged, and the more failures, the more damage.

Regulatory compliance and risk management appear to go hand in hand. The best companies have always addressed strategic risk from the boardroom; Basel 2 and today's corporate governance regimes increasingly expect risk management to be pervasive throughout the culture of all organizations.

UK Combined Code and Turnbull Guidance

The UK's Combined Code requires listed companies to review annually 'all material controls, including financial, operational and compliance controls, and risk management systems'.[8] The Turnbull Guidance explicitly requires boards, on an ongoing basis, to identify, assess and deal with significant risks in all areas, including in information and communications processes.[9]

Sarbanes-Oxley

The Sarbanes-Oxley Act of 2002 ('SOX') requires US-listed companies to assess annually the effectiveness of their internal controls, for the CEO and CFO to certify annually the adequacy of internal controls, and for the external auditors to attest this. Section 409 requires companies to notify the SEC 'on a rapid and current basis such additional information concerning material changes in the financial condition or operations of the issuer'.

These governance regimes – particularly Sarbanes-Oxley – have substantial IT compliance components.

Authorities are increasingly looking to regulation to force the issue up the corporate agenda:

> 'The road to information security goes through corporate governance. America cannot solve its cyber security challenges by delegating them to government officials or CIOs. The best way to strengthen US information security

---

8 *Combined Code on Corporate Governance*, Section C.2.1, July 2003 (*www.fsa.gov.uk/pubs/ukla/lr_comcode 2003.pdf*).

9 'Turnbull Guidance', paragraph 21.

is to treat it as a corporate governance issue that requires the attention of boards and CEOs.'[10]

Information risk

Organizational information is an asset and therefore, by definition, someone outside the organization will want it; if no-one wanted it, it wouldn't be an asset. Information, to be useful to an organization, must be

- available (to those who need to use it),

- confidential (so that competitors can't use it) and

- its integrity must be guaranteed (so that it can be relied upon).

Information risk arises from the threats – originating both externally and internally – to the availability, confidentiality and integrity of the organization's information assets.

Headline figures illustrate the cost of security failures: the UK's National High Tech Crime Unit (NHTCU) reported[11] that 89% of firms interviewed had suffered some form of computer crime in the previous 12 months (up from 83% in the previous year), at a cost of at least £2.4 billion.

Threats to information security are wide-ranging, complex and costly. External threats include:

- casual criminals (virus writers, hackers),

- organized crime (virus writers, hackers, spammers, fraudsters, espionage, ex-employees) and

---

10 US National Cyber Security Summit Task Force, 'Information Security Governance: a Call to Action', April 2004 (*www.hipaadvisory.com/action/security/Info SecGov4_04.pdf*).

11 'Hi-Tech Crime: the Impact on UK Business 2005', survey conducted by NOP for the UK's NHTCU.

- terrorists (including anarchists).

Securing information against organized crime and cyber terrorism should be high on corporate agendas.

More information security incidents (involving members of staff, contractors and consultants acting either maliciously or carelessly) originate inside the organization than outside it. White-collar crime is, nowadays, largely computer-based. Baring, Enron, WorldCom and Arthur Andersen were all brought down by insiders.

The indirect costs of information security incidents usually far exceed their direct ones, and the reputational impacts are often even greater.

Project governance

Organizations continuously upgrade their systems or deploy new systems to improve customer service, reduce cost, improve product or service quality, and to deliver new products, services and business models. These deployments often involve strategic risk for the organization; they always involve operational risk.

Risk management is a board responsibility and, therefore, project governance – from inception through to deployment – must also be a board responsibility.

IT projects are not always delivered successfully. Authoritative research shows that the majority of projects fail to deliver the benefits that justified commencing the project and that, of those that do, the majority come in late and/or over budget.

Organizations whose IT projects failed usually all deployed recognizable project management methodologies; the reasons for failure were invariably to do with failures of project governance rather than simply of operational management.

Increasingly, shareholders are concerned about project failure. In the past, investment analysts were reluctant to assess IT. Institutional shareholders are now becoming more muscular.

Technology is as significant a component of the organization's cost base as its headcount, but usually consumes substantially more capital.

Driven, in part, by the changing corporate governance climate and, in equal part, by the poor record of IT projects, stakeholders and institutional shareholders increasingly seek transparency around IT.

The Standish Group's research on IT project failure[12] found that:

- 16.2% of software projects were completed on time and on budget;

- 31% of projects were cancelled before completion; and

- 53% of projects would cost over 189% of their original estimates.

More recent surveys indicate that nothing much has changed.

But it's not only about project failure: 80% of corporate assets today are digital[13] and, as shareholders and boards focus on the extent to which information and intellectual capital are fundamental to their competitive position and long-term survival, so they recognize the fiduciary nature of their responsibility to shareholders in respect of the organization's information assets and IT.

As they recognize the impact that technology has on business performance (and, consequently, on shareholder value), so they look increasingly for a framework which ensures that IT projects are aligned with commercial objectives and which

---

12 'The Chaos Report', The Standish Group, 1994.

13 Testimony of Jody R Westby, PwC Managing Director, to the House of Congress Committee on Government Reform, September 2004.

enables companies to quantify and report in a consistent manner on IT investments.[14]

IT investment decisions (for *or* against) expose an organization to significant risk: strategic, financial, operational and competitive. The pace of change is a significant risk. Project risks must be assessed within the organization's strategic planning and risk management framework for the right decision, one which enhances competitive advantage and delivers measurable value, to be made. Critically, projects need continual oversight; the assumptions on which they were predicated need continual re-assessment and the expected benefits need regular re-appraisal.

---

14 HP IT Governance Roundtable, 24 October 2002.

CHAPTER 4: SYMPTOMS OF INADEQUATE IT GOVERNANCE

1. How does your board assess (measure) the real contribution made by any of your IT systems to improving the organization's competitiveness?

2. What divergence is there between the views that your sales/operational management has of the benefits of IT systems and projects and those of the IT management? Who is right and how do you find out? Are you getting maximum value (maximum business benefit for minimum actual total cost) for each of your IT investments? How would you know? How would you know if your IT spending is putting your company at a cost disadvantage?

3. What is your board's process for comparing the (fully costed) ROI on your technology projects to those of any other strategic options, including acquisitions, and how does this affect strategic planning?

4. What is your board's view on the relationship, in your organization, between the potential impact of a compliance or information security failure (in financial terms) and the (fully absorbed) cost of meeting the compliance and security objectives? What is the total actual (direct and indirect) cost of all the compliance and information security incidents in your organization in the last twelve months?

5. What is the real, financial value to your organization of its information and intellectual capital and how are you leveraging it?

6. How are you driving up the intellectual capital/headcount ratio? What's the relationship between this ratio and the IT intensity (IT investment to headcount) ratio?

7. Do all your IT projects come in on time, to budget and to specification?

8. How does your D&O insurance deal with the personal consequences for directors of IT failures arising from inadequate board oversight of core business processes and significant financial transactions?

If you organization has a clear, widely understood set of answers to these questions, complete with meaningful metrics, then you have an effective IT governance framework in place. Very few organizations do.

CHAPTER 5: WHAT IS AN IT GOVERNANCE FRAMEWORK?

An IT governance framework consists, essentially, of a set of principles, a decision-making hierarchy and a tailor-made suite of reporting and monitoring processes.

There are eight key decision areas for designing an IT governance framework:

1. IT governance principles and decision-making hierarchy. There are two types of principle in this context:

   a. governance principles, to do with how IT is to be managed in the enterprise, and

   b. implementation principles, to do with how IT is to be used to achieve the business strategy.

2. The information strategy (which must be derived from the business strategy):

   a. What information do we need, where does it come from and what are we going to do with it?

   b. Out of the information strategy comes the ICT strategy, which is made up of:

      i. application,

      ii. architecture, and

      iii. infrastructure/technology strategies.

3. IT risk management – within the context of the organization's overall risk management framework, risk to information and ICT needs to be treated in line with organization-wide criteria. These criteria should be reflected in the controls developed as part of the IT governance framework and the reporting and monitoring processes.

4. Software applications – how business applications are specified, developed, authorized, acquired, managed.

5. ICT architecture – including the integration and standardization requirements – that will meet the requirements of the information and applications strategy.

6. ICT infrastructure/technology:

   a. How are IT services (including hardware and communications protocols) specified, developed, authorized, acquired and managed?

   b. What services should be outsourced, how, why and to whom?

7. ICT investment and project governance – given the ICT strategy,

   a. which IT initiatives (including outsourcing initiatives) should be implemented?

   b. how should they be prioritized?

   c. how should they be project managed?

   d. what returns should be expected?

   e. how should the portfolio of projects be managed?

   f. how should any resultant business change be managed?

8. Information compliance and security:

   a. What are the criteria for securing information?

   b. How do we demonstrate legal/regulatory compliance?

   c. How should this be measured and demonstrated?

   d. How is IP protected?

   e. What audits are required?

IT steering committee

IT governance is as much about IT leadership as anything else. The board needs to create a mechanism through which it can provide the business with technology leadership. Technology or IT leadership requires a specific mechanism, in a way that, for instance, neither HR (Human Resources) nor Sales do, for two reasons:

1. HR, sales, marketing, etc, are usually already dealt with effectively as part of the existing board agenda; most board members already understand the issues around sales and marketing and the people involved in making sales happen already get a great deal of informed attention. The organization almost certainly already has well-developed governance frameworks for these key activities. No additional benefits would accrue to the organization through the creation of additional leadership mechanisms for these activities.

2. IT, in contrast, is not as well understood at board level and there are usually no established IT governance frameworks inside organizations. It is not well understood, but it is critical: on average, investment in IT represents more than 50% of every organization's annual capital investment and, typically, more than 30% of its cost base is in IT – for most businesses, the direct cost of IT operations is now second only to staffing as an expense item. There is, in other words, a gap between the importance of IT and the understanding of IT: an IT governance framework closes that gap, providing all those with a limited understanding of IT in the enterprise with a framework within which they can improve their understanding to a level appropriate for this critical contributor to their competitive position.

The board-level IT steering or strategy committee has a number of functions, some of which (depending on the size, structure and complexity of the organization) may be dealt with through sub-committees.

This committee takes the lead in dealing with IT governance principles (including the decision-making hierarchy), strategy and risk treatment criteria. The board also has a key monitoring and oversight role across the whole of IT, and particularly in respect of project governance. This monitoring component means that the board IT committee has similarities to the audit committee and, given the extent to which IT governance issues impinge on audit issues (particularly around internal control, eg, Sarbanes-Oxley) there is some sense in having a number of members of each committee in common.

They are not the same committees though. In some organizations the monitoring component of the IT governance framework will be included in the agenda of the audit committee, in order to ensure a clear segregation between those responsible for determining the ICT strategy of the organization and approving investment, and those responsible for monitoring and overseeing the appropriateness and effectiveness of those decisions.

Composition of the IT steering committee

The composition of the board steering committee should be straightforward. The chair should be selected on exactly the same basis, following the same rules, as the chair of the audit committee. There should be a majority of outside directors on the committee, and key executives should be invited to attend: the CEO, the CFO and the CIO (or equivalent) would be included as a minimum. In some organizations, it would be appropriate to include the CCO (Chief Compliance Officer) as well.

The other key business heads in the organization (whether production, procurement, retail, sales, marketing, etc, depends on the sector, the organization and the existing management structure) – the ones who would be included in any business strategy committee – should be included in the IT steering committee.

The CIO's position and level of accountability should be clear. The CIO should be on the same level, and have the same status, as the CFO and the other functional heads (eg, sales, marketing, etc), with direct responsibility for managing the IT operations and personal accountability for the success of organizational IT activity.

1. The IT steering committee needs at least one outside director who has the right mix of business and IT experience and sufficient gravitas to lead the board's IT governance efforts.

2. All the other directors should be prepared and determined to question every aspect of IT planning and activity.

3. The executive – particularly the CIO and the IT management – should be banned from using IT jargon, and forced to express everything they have to say about IT in a format that focuses on comprehensible (to the non-IT specialist) opportunities, issues, risks or plans.

4. Employ outside experts (strategic IT consultants) as board advisers with the specific brief of confirming that what the board has been told is accurate, complete and true and, if not, what has been left out.

Enterprise IT architecture committee

A critical component of a useful IT governance framework is the enterprise IT architecture. The determination of this architecture can only take place in the context of the business and information strategies, in line with the key IT implementation principles and taking the security, compliance and risk treatment criteria into account.

The enterprise IT architecture is a set of organizing principles that determine the way in which the organization's information and communications technology will interact with its operating systems, applications and data.

The architecture should (for instance, if the key principles adopted allow it) ensure technical integration, minimising inter-system hand-offs (which is where significant cost and risk reside) and allowing the IT organization to cost-effectively respond to businesses needs.

The ongoing role of this committee is to ensure that all ICT deployments (including outsourcing proposals) are in line with it, fiercely warding off attempts to deploy non-standard hardware or systems – unless the architecture itself is adapted, taking into account the ramifications for existing installations, future upgrades and current projects.

This committee might, in larger organizations, be led by a Chief Architect, who would also be responsible for the formalization and communication across the organization of the architecture.

Key members of the committee, alongside business delegates who understand the organizational architecture, would include senior managers with expertise in systems, data, security and infrastructure. The organizational risk manager should also be involved with this committee.

IT audit

The second area in which most organizations are inadequate, where IT is concerned, is oversight. 'Oversight' must include oversight by the board and must cover more than internal financial controls. Every board needs to empower either the IT Committee or the Audit Committee to deal with IT oversight.

An IT audit plan needs, just like a financial audit plan, to reflect the organization's key risk areas. It must review regulatory compliance, information security, IT project progress and technical implementation, as well as the skills and competences of the specialized staff employed in the organization.

Its objective is to provide the outside directors with real, technical assurance that the IT implementation principles and the governance framework are being applied, and to identify any areas of non-conformance that need to be drawn to the attention of directors.

Use qualified IT auditors for this work, and insist that they work within your organization's risk and IT governance framework. Pay no attention to non-conformance reports that are based on anything other than your own framework.

Third-party standards

There are a number[15] of information- and IT-related external management standards that an organization may choose, be required or be mandated to deploy. The best known and most widely used are:

- CoBIT (Control Objectives for Information and Related Technology), which is 'increasingly internationally accepted as good practice for control over information,

---

15 See, in this Pocket Book series, *IT Governance Frameworks*, and *Information Security Frameworks.*

IT and related risks. Its guidance enables an enterprise to implement effective governance over IT'.[16]

- AS 8015-2005, the Australian standard for the corporate governance of information and communication technology.

- COSO (Committee of Sponsoring Organizations of the Treadway Commission) – an integrated framework for internal control.

- GAISP (Generally Accepted Information Security Principles) – a failed attempt to unify and harmonize information security principles and to measure their success.

- ISO 17799:2005 (the international code of best practice for information security) and ISO27001:2005 (against which an organization's information security management system can be certified as conforming.

- ITIL (IT Infrastructure Library) – an integrated set of best practice recommendations for IT management. ISO 20000 is the international standard for IT service management and is heavily based on ITIL.

Each of these management systems is sponsored by a different organization and, while there is substantial overlap, each has a slightly different objective and none provides a complete IT governance framework. CoBIT or COSO, for instance, are important for Sarbanes-Oxley compliance but may be more than organizations in many other jurisdictions require immediately.

ISO 27001 is increasingly important for organizations seeking to win outsourcing contracts, particularly those to do with call centres and other activities dealing with personal information. In many jurisdictions, the fact of conformity with a management system such as ISO 27001 will be taken as

---

16 www.isaca.org.

evidence that the board has properly discharged its responsibilities in respect of information security and data protection.

External systems are all useful, if you identify those that you actually need and you ensure they are effectively integrated. Other systems and standards – such as CMMI and six sigma – are also important, and individual industry sectors (eg, healthcare, financial services) sometimes have their own specific requirements around information security and internal control.

The IT governance framework has to be designed in such a way that, where more than one of these systems is required, they are successfully and – to the greatest extent possible – seamlessly integrated.

CHAPTER 6: BENEFITS OF AN IT GOVERNANCE FRAMEWORK

Good governance only makes sense if it makes sense. As long ago as 1996, McKinsey and Company found that two-thirds of the companies in a survey would pay an 11% premium for the stock of a company with good governance practices.[17]

More than that, 'companies whose boards engage in one or more of [the] three governance practices that signal board independence from management outperform their peers and produce higher returns for their shareholders',[18] as measured by economic value added (EVA – earnings (post-tax) in excess of the cost of the capital required to generate them).

And if good governance makes sense, good IT governance makes even more sense:

'[T]op-performing firms succeed where others fail by implementing effective IT governance to support their strategies. Firms with above-average IT governance following a specific strategy... had more than 20 percent higher profits than firms with poor governance following the same strategy.'[19]

Research by Weill and Ross also indicates that 'top-performing enterprises generate returns on their investments up to 40 percent greater than their competitors'.[20]

---

17 Ned Regan, 'Entrepreneurial Companies, Strong Boards and Shareholder Value', *Corporate Board Member Magazine*, August 2002.

18 'The Active Board of Directors and Improved Performance of the Large Publicly Traded Corporation', Millstein and MacAvoy.

19 Peter D Weill and Jeanne W Ross, *IT Governance: How Top Performers Manage IT Decision Rights for Superior Results*, Harvard Business School Press, 2004.

20 Ibid.

An IT governance framework is an integral and essential component of the value-focused twenty-first century organization's overall governance approach. The development, deployment and integration into its total governance structure of such a framework, though, does far more than simply ensure that the board is complying with both the spirit and the letter of current and emerging national and international corporate governance requirements.

It does more than give boards and directors a reliable defence, in commercial or regulatory legal actions, that they took reasonable steps to deploy identified best practice for protecting and enhancing corporate information and intellectual assets, managing risk, controlling IT investment and complying with information and computer-related regulation.

The key benefit of an effective, integrated IT governance framework is the leap forward in competitiveness that is achieved through the complete integration of IT into the strategic and operational management approach of the organization. Survival in the information economy is hard without integrating IT governance into the overall corporate governance structure; long-term success is impossible.

CHAPTER 7: THE CALDER-MOIR IT GOVERNANCE FRAMEWORK

The Calder-Moir IT Governance Framework[21] is a straightforward framework for structuring IT governance within an organization.

The IT Governance Framework

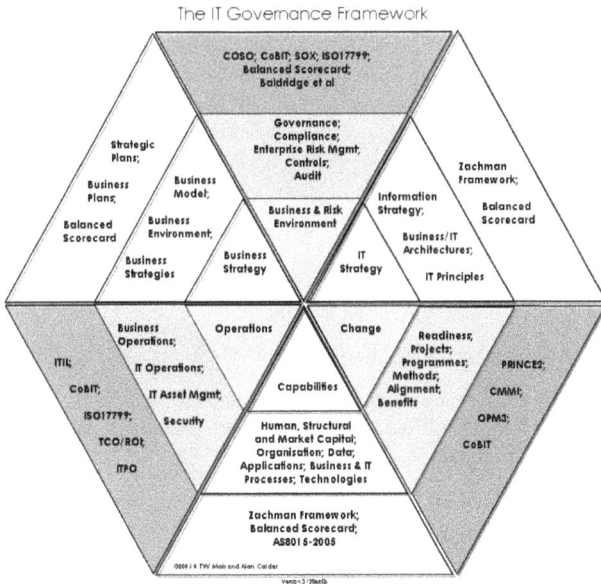

21 The IT Governance Framework – Toolkit is a comprehensive set of tools and templates that support the development and deployment of an IT governance framework in an organization. Copies can be purchased from: www.itgovernance.co.uk/products/519.

Most of the IT-related disciplines offer solutions and tools that can help with IT governance, but most of them are very detailed, and have narrow scopes. No single tool provides a full picture of IT governance, and collectively they can give a confusing picture that hinders the purpose of IT governance, which is to equip boards with information and levers for directing, evaluating and monitoring how well IT supports their core business.

The Calder-Moir Framework is not another solution, but a way of organizing IT governance issues and tools to support the board, executives and practitioners. It places IT governance tools in the context of an end-to-end process, and provides a simple reference point for discussing the many aspects of IT direction and performance.

The framework consists of six segments, each of which represents one step in the end-to-end process that starts with business strategy and finishes with IT operational support for delivery of business value against that strategy.

Each segment is divided into three layers:

- The innermost layer represents the board, which directs, evaluates and monitors information technology support for business.

- The middle layer represents executive management, which is responsible for managing the activities that deliver the end-to-end process.

- The outermost layer represents the IT practitioners and IT governance practitioners, who use proven tools and methodologies to plan, design, assess, control and deliver the IT support for business.

Navigating the framework

The top half of the framework covers the processes that establish direction, specify constraints, make decisions and plan.

The bottom half covers the processes that develop new capabilities, manage the capabilities and use IT to deliver business products and services.

Start at the '9 o'clock' position (business strategy), and follow the segments clockwise through the end-to-end process:

The board decides the organisation's goals and business strategies. These are analysed and designed by the executive managers and their strategy practitioners. The strategies must operate within one or more corporate governance regimes (the Combined Code, Sarbanes-Oxley, Basel 2 and so on.

They also operate within a risk environment, so it is critical to undertake a thorough risk assessment to decide which controls will be the most appropriate. The first two segments, then, describe the organization's path and desired outcomes, the constraints within which it must operate, and the controls that will be most appropriate in those contexts.

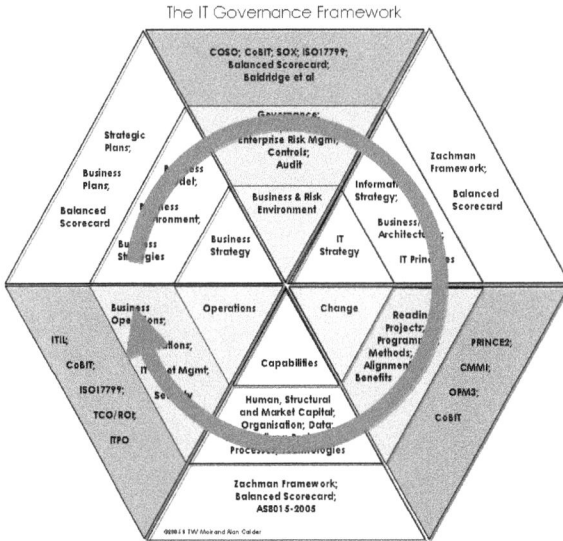

The IT Governance Framework

Once the business strategies, governance regimes, risk assessment and controls have been developed, IT works with the business to develop architectures and plans to deliver on those requirements. The result is a set of proposals and plans that describe what business and IT should look like, the expected performance, the changes required to deliver that performance, and the resource implications. IT governance processes verify that the proposals meet the business strategy and corporate governance requirements (including risk management and controls), and help the board to evaluate the merits of the plans and proposals.

After the board approves the plans and proposals, they can be implemented through a series of change projects – subject to regular monitoring within the IT governance regime, including controls developed by the risk assessment process. The projects create or update the organization's business and IT capabilities, which should then meet the performance and control criteria established during the planning phases. The capabilities are then deployed into business and IT operations for delivery of products and services – again governed by the performance and control criteria.

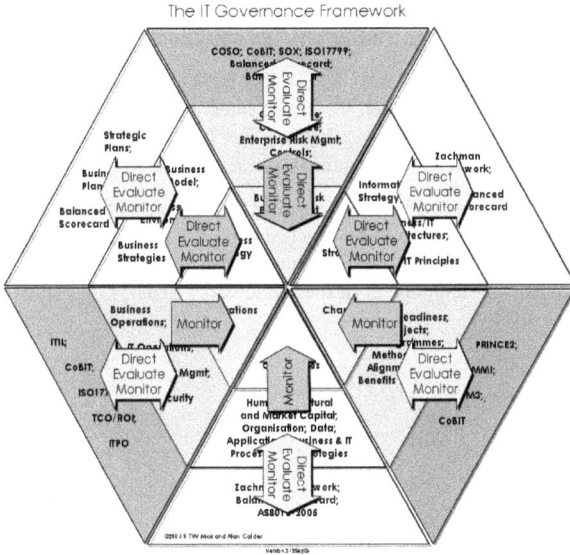

The IT Governance Framework

Evaluate, direct, monitor

The Australian standard AS8015-2005 (Corporate Governance of Information and Communication Technology) identifies three main IT governance tasks for directors:

- evaluate,
- direct, and
- monitor.

The board evaluates the business conditions, strategies, constraints and IT proposals. It directs by guiding the way IT should be used (IT principles), the appropriate risk and compliance posture, and the investment in IT proposals. And it monitors all processes in the Calder-Moir hexagon – business strategy, the business and risk environment (and constraints), IT strategy, change, capabilities and operations.

If any of these processes fails – that is, doesn't deliver exactly what is required – then the board intervenes (directs) through the processes in the top half of the framework, refining or reinforcing the guidelines for business and IT.

Similarly, executive managers direct, evaluate, and monitor the processes carried out by practitioners, but are – for obvious reasons – more closely involved than the directors in all activities in both halves of the framework.

APPENDIX: IT GOVERNANCE RESOURCES

IT Governance Ltd source, create and deliver products and services to meet the real-world, evolving IT governance needs of today's organizations, directors, managers and practitioners. The ITG website (*www.itgovernance.co.uk*) is *the* international one-stop-shop for corporate and IT governance information, advice, guidance, books, tools, training and consultancy.

www.27001.com is the IT Governance Ltd website that deals specifically with information security issues in a North American context.

Pocket Guides

For full details of the entire range of Pocket Guides, listed below, simply follow the links at *www.itgovernance.co.uk/page.publishing*.

Practical Information Security Pocket Guides

- A Dictionary of Information Security Terms, Abbreviations and Acronyms
- ISO 27001 Assessment without tears
- ISO 27001: a Pocket Guide
- Risk Assessments for Asset Owners

Practical IT Governance Pocket Guides
- Enterprise Architecture
- Information Governance
- Information Security Governance
- IT Audit
- IT Governance
- IT Governance Frameworks
- IT regulatory compliance in the UK
- Project Governance
- The Integrated Management System

Practical Governance Pocket Guides
- BASEL 2
- Business Continuity
- Corporate Governance in the UK (Turnbull)
- Corporate Governance in the US (Sarbanes-Oxley)
- Enterprise Risk Management (ERM)
- Operational Risk

Toolkits

ITG's unique range of toolkits includes the IT Governance Framework Toolkit, which contains all the tools and guidance that you will need in order to develop and implement an appropriate IT governance framework for your organization. Full details can be found at *www.itgovernance.co.uk/products/519*.

For a free paper on how to use the proprietary CALDER-MOIR IT Governance Framework, and for a free trial version of the toolkit, see *www.itgovernance.co.uk/page.framework*.

Newsletter

IT governance is one of the hottest topics in business today, not least because it is also the fastest-moving, so what better way to keep up than by subscribing to ITG's free monthly newsletter, *Sentinel*? It provides monthly updates and resources across the whole spectrum of IT governance subject matter, including risk management, information security, ITIL and IT service management, project governance, compliance and so much more. Subscribe for your free copy at: *www.itgovernance.co.uk/newsletter.aspx*.

EU for product safety is Stephen Evans, The Mill Enterprise Hub, Stagreenan, Drogheda, Co. Louth, A92 CD3D, Ireland. (servicecentre@itgovernance.eu)

www.ingramcontent.com/pod-product-compliance
Lightning Source LLC
Chambersburg PA
CBHW071126210326
41519CB00020B/6432